EXPLORING
THEATER

Set Design and Prop Making in Theater

Bethany Bryan

Cavendish
Square

New York

Published in 2017 by Cavendish Square Publishing, LLC
243 5th Avenue, Suite 136, New York, NY 10016

CPSIA Compliance Information: Batch #CW17CSQ

All websites were available and accurate when this book was sent to press.

Library of Congress Cataloging-in-Publication Data

Names: Bryan, Bethany.
Title: Set design and prop making in theater / Bethany Bryan .
Description: New York : Cavendish Square Publishing, 2017. | Series: Exploring theater | Includes index.
Identifiers: ISBN 9781502622792 (library bound) | ISBN 9781502622808 (ebook)
Subjects: LCSH: Stage props--Juvenile literature. | Theaters--Stage-setting and scenery--Juvenile literature.
Classification: LCC PN2091.S8 B78 2017 | DDC 792'.025--dc23

Editorial Director: David McNamara
Editor: Fletcher Doyle
Copy Editor: Nathan Heidelberger
Associate Art Director: Amy Greenan
Designer: Jessica Nevins
Production Coordinator: Karol Szymczuk
Photo Research: J8 Media

The photographs in this book are used by permission and through the courtesy of: Cover Pxel/Alamy Stock Photo; p. 4 Charles Cook/Lonely Planet/Images/Getty Images; p. 9 Syda Productions/Shutterstock.com; p. 11 Jim West/Alamy Stock Photo; p. 14 wutzkohphoto/Shutterstock.com; p. 16 Jupiterimages/Photolibrary/Getty Images; p. 21 Gary Gershoff/WireImage/Getty Images; p. 27 Manfred Schmid/Getty Images; p. 30 John Burke/Stockbyte/Getty Images; p. 32 GOLFX/Shutterstock.com; p. 35 CRAIG LASSIG/AFP/Getty Images; p. 40 Zoran Milich/Photonica World/Getty Images; p. 42 Pxel/Alamy Stock Photo; p. 45 Robert Kneschke/Shutterstock.com; p. 47 wavebreakmedia/Shutterstock.com; p. 49 courtesy of Michael Krikorian; p. 51 ITAR-TASS Photo Agency/Alamy Stock Photo; p. 55 Hemera Technologies/AbleStock.com/Thinkstock; p. 57 Steve Raymer/Corbis Documentary/Getty Images; p. 61 Jakez/Shutterstock.com; p. 62 Geraint Lewis/Alamy Stock Photo; p. 66 Allan Grant/The LIFE Picture Collection/Getty Images; p. 70 John Snelling/Getty Images; p. 72 Paul Wood/Alamy Stock Photo; p. 75 Adam Gregor/Shutterstock.com; p. 76 Jupiterimages/BananaStock/Thinkstock; p. 79 Kartinkin77/Shutterstock.com; p. 81 ROBYN BECK/AFP/Getty Images; p. 86 Andrew Nicholson/Alamy Stock Photo; p. 87 Syda Productions/Shutterstock.com.

Printed in the United States of America

CONTENTS

The stage is set for a production at the Steppenwolf Theatre in Chicago. What can you infer about the lives of the characters, based on the props and set design displayed here?

CHAPTER ONE

THE RIGHT STUFF

Y ou're drawn to the theater department at your school. However, you aren't ready to be on stage. You aren't sure about your singing or acting skills. You are creative and want to get involved, but you aren't sure where you fit in. There are many jobs that need to be done to put on a successful show. One of the most critical is planning, designing, and building props and sets that help to bring the audience into the performance and engage the imagination. This book is here to help you figure out if this is the right path for you.

Props and Sets

When you enter a theater before the performance of a play or musical, often you'll see that the curtains are open and you're able to see the stage. What do you see? A living room that looks an awful lot like yours? A worn couch? A laundry basket? Or maybe you see an outdoor picnic area with a table all set for dinner, and lawn chairs, and a place for a campfire. Or is it something less cut and dried? Maybe you see an empty stage with only a few chairs in the middle. Or there could be several large wooden platforms in front of a red satin **backdrop**. No matter how simple or elaborate what you see onstage is, a lot of thought and care was put into what you see when you enter the theater and when the performance begins. How this changes (if it changes) over the course of the performance works hand-in-hand with the actors' performances, the lighting, the sound, the costumes, and more. Determining the set design and the part that props should play in the performance is the role of the **set designer**, **props master**, **head carpenter**, and crewmembers and assistants. They help design, build, paint, create, manage, and find all of the materials necessary to bring a performance to life.

One of the most important aspects of staging a theater performance is setting the scene. Does the play or musical take place on a dusty ranch in 1870s America? Or in Victorian England? Or at the bottom of the ocean three thousand years into the future? The props and sets convey any of these possibilities to the audience.

Sourcing and creating props for a performance can take you from a thrift store to a fabric store to a camping store and everywhere in between. Designing and building a set can involve everything from carpentry to papier-mâché. Whether you have the soul of a builder or the heart of an artist, you can play an active role in creating what the audience sees on stage.

The Skills You Need

One popular misconception about theater is that you have to have an obvious talent in order to be involved. The primary trait you need to possess initially in order to take part in your school's theater program and beyond is a passion for theater. Maybe you saw a performance of *Les Misérables* that you haven't been able to forget. Perhaps you were specifically drawn to the towering sets that flawlessly recreated Paris in the early to mid-1800s. Maybe you were captivated by a performance of *Fun Home* and the vintage props that you felt brought you into a living room in the 1970s. New plays and musicals are being written and produced every day. Sets and **special effects** are becoming more elaborate as technology makes that possible. If that idea excites you, you have a passion for theater. So, congratulations! You have the desire that you need. However, if you want to be successful at it and help your fellow classmates put on the most amazing performance of their lives, there are a few more skills that come into play.

- **A willingness to learn.** At a high school level, the roles of set designer, props master, and head carpenter will likely be performed by teachers or parent volunteers. But this is your chance to watch, learn, and ask questions. If you have worked with tools and have experience painting, you can make a major contribution to the show while observing how to lead a crew. But when you're starting out, it's important to open your mind and just

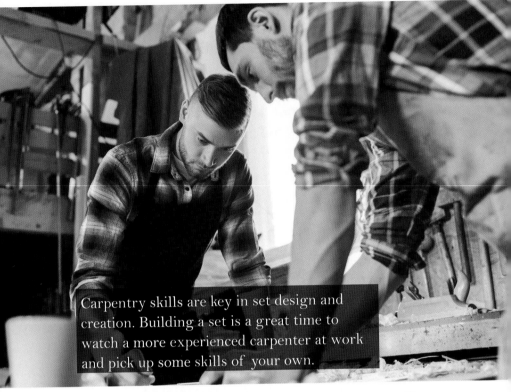

Carpentry skills are key in set design and creation. Building a set is a great time to watch a more experienced carpenter at work and pick up some skills of your own.

display a good attitude toward learning. You might pick up some carpentry skills you didn't have before, or learn how to paint material to create the illusion that it is something else.

- **Research skills.** The ability to research architecture, furniture, and objects used in various times in history is very necessary for someone involved in creating sets and props. Part of making realistic props and authentic sets is to make them look as they did in the period in which the play is set. For example, if the play calls for a sword, you must find out if the blades used at that time were long, thin, curved, or double-edged. If you have good research skills, you can be a good resource for the team.

- **Creativity.** Creativity comes in many forms. One form is the ability to think of ways to use discarded materials so that props and sets can be built inexpensively. There are many examples in the blog *The Art of Faking It— Stage Design, Themed Rooms, Props, and More* (bigpicturecreations.blogspot.com). In one, the author demonstrates how to create the architectural details of a Brooklyn brownstone using pieces of 1-inch (2.5-centimeter) Styrofoam cut out using a template and then glued together. There are painting tips to create the illusion of stone. Large pieces of Styrofoam can be found at appliance stores; they are thrown out after stoves and refrigerators are unpacked. So whether your creativity comes in the form of painting, finding ways to turn scraps of material into usable props, or planning elaborate video game battles, be prepared to bring it to the table. It also helps to have an eye for detail.

- **Communication and listening skills.** No matter whether you're leading a crew as part of a multimillion-dollar theater production on Broadway or painting a backdrop for a junior high production of *The Sound of Music*, the listening and communication skills you bring to the table are invaluable. A theater production is driven by teamwork, and it's important to keep everyone informed and to know when to ask questions. Treat rehearsals and meetings the same way you do a class that interests you. Take notes! You should keep a notebook on hand— or even an electronic tablet with a note-taking app. Use these tools to sketch ideas and write down pertinent questions to ask later.

- **Organization.** A theater production can take weeks or months to plan. And on opening night, the cast and crew rely on every prop being in place and every piece of the set being in working order. Otherwise, a performance can go off the rails pretty quickly! So it's important to be

When preparing for a production, you'll have a chance to get to know the other members of the crew. Teamwork gets the work done more efficiently.

organized. If you're the type of student who keeps color-coded notes for every class and a spreadsheet of homework deadlines, then you already know how to keep track of things. But even if organization skills don't come naturally to you, the theater is a great place to hone them.

- **Active involvement.** It's not enough to simply sign up to participate in a theater production. You have to actively be involved. This means showing up to every rehearsal and showing up on time. You must be able to meet deadlines while working under pressure. Volunteer to be a part of a particular crew, and be prepared to work hard until the final show is over and the set has been struck.

It's Time to Participate!

So, you've decided you want to get involved in theater and have some skills to contribute to a production. What now? First, check out what's available at your school. Does your school have a **drama club**? Are they planning a production? Maybe the music department and theater program are combining to stage a musical. If work is already under way, that's okay! There are a lot of options out there if you're willing to look for them. Your town might have a **community theater**. Check online for community theater groups.

If your school has a drama club or other theater program, then sign up. If you're shy and feel a lot of trepidation, talk a friend into signing up, too. Once you get to know the other drama club members, you might even feel your shyness begin to melt away. If your interest is specifically in sets and props, be sure to let the club president or student advisor know. Ask how you can be involved, specifically, in those departments.

What You'll Learn

One thing that almost every theater student or theater professional will tell you is that it's a learning experience. And you take those skills with you, whether it's to a career in theater or another type of job. Let's take a look at some of the skills you'll gain and how they'll affect your life as a student and into your career and beyond.

Improvisation and Problem Solving

Whether you're onstage or behind the curtain during a performance, when something goes wrong, everyone has to do a lot of quick thinking to make it right. An actor might drop a prop off the edge of the stage, where it breaks. As a props master, it's your job to find a fast replacement and get it into the actor's hand without him leaving the stage. Do you have a backup ready to go? Can you find one within thirty seconds? Quick thinking is a skill that you learn to use during times like these and one you take with you for the rest of your life, or even just to the next time your teacher surprises you with a quiz.

Project Management and Leadership

Whether you're part of a Broadway production or a high school theater performance, in order to work as a team, you'll need strong, effective leadership. You might eventually be given that role. Being able to manage a crew and prepare for a performance is something that helps prepare you for assuming leadership in your future roles as a parent or a manager in your career field.

Working Within a Budget

No matter the size of your production, putting on a theater performance costs money. In a leadership role in the theater, part of your job is planning a show on a sometimes-impossible **budget**. Set your budget priorities and stick to them, then get creative in finding cheap solutions for your other needs. Budgeting for expenses is something you'll do in your personal life and likely your professional life.

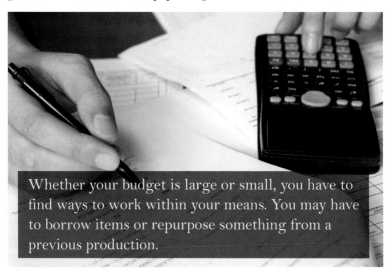

Whether your budget is large or small, you have to find ways to work within your means. You may have to borrow items or repurpose something from a previous production.

Dealing with Lots of Different People

In the theater, you'll be around a lot of different types of people. Some people are bossy. Some people are shy. Some people are good at leading others, and some aren't. How you interact with all different types of people will prepare you for the future. You might one day have a difficult boss who has trouble communicating his or her needs to you, but because you experienced something similar with a director long ago, you'll know how to handle the situation effectively.

Finding Your Niche

Some people crave the limelight, and other people like being behind the scenes. Others aren't sure just yet. You might feel shy in class, but once you step on the stage, you want to sing and dance and don't care who's watching. Friends might push you to try out for a lead role when what you really want to do is run the lights or take charge of the entire production in a leadership role. Perhaps you already feel a pull toward set design or props and are excited to get started drawing out your plans for your school's next theater production. And maybe after a few weeks on a crew building a set, you'll realize that you'd rather be in the limelight after all. And that's OK! It's exciting to try out some different jobs until you find your **niche**. Your niche, put simply, is something you're good at that makes you happy. It might take you a few days or a few years to find it, but being involved in theater will help you find it.

No matter your ultimate goal, the best thing to do is to just jump in see where it takes you. Join the drama club. Check out your town's community theater. Get involved! You'll be glad you did.

When watching a scene from *Hamlet*, you don't often think about the props department that found or made the skull to whom Hamlet delivers one of his most famous speeches.

CHAPTER TWO

TEAMWORK AND THEATER

In act 5, scene 1 of *Hamlet*, Hamlet delivers his famous speech while holding the skull of Yorick, a long-dead court jester who Hamlet once knew and fondly remembers. The scene is very sad and powerful (and more than a little disturbing). No matter which actor is playing the role of Hamlet, whether it be Jude Law, Kenneth Branagh, or your classmate, the scene just wouldn't work without a realistic skull. In the planning stages of the production, a member of the crew had to find or make a believable, lifelike skull, someone else had to place it within the actor's reach at exactly the right moment, and then another crew member had to keep track of the skull, put it in a safe place, and get it all ready for the next performance. To do all of those things requires organization, creativity, and teamwork. That's the theater in a nutshell. Every head of every department, every crewmember, every cast member, the director, the producer, even the person taking tickets at the box office, must work in unison to pull off a performance.

Here are some of the roles and responsibilities that go into creating the props and sets of a theater production.

Set Design 101

According to the American Association of Community Theatre (AACT), a set designer is the individual who "designs the physical surroundings in which the action will take place." This task helps to reflect the **mood** of the characters onstage, clues the audience in to the time period and location in which the story unfolds, and even just hides the action **backstage** (or the actors and crew) from the audience. A set designer might sketch out the layout of the stage, detailing the placement of props or set components, or even build miniatures to help lay out the plan effectively. A set designer works alongside the director and the show's design team to talk about the director's vision for the performance. A set designer will also meet with the lighting team and costume department to help create a sense of unity onstage.

Set Design Styles

A set design can be brought to life in a number of different styles, and that style affects how audience members interpret the performance. According to an entry on the *Big Picture Creations* blog, "Stage design is not just creating a place for the actors, performers, characters, speakers to walk on, but to interact with, a place that is their home. It is important to keep this in mind while designing a set for a production—it has to represent them."

Some set designers prefer to work in a realistic style. **Realism** allows the set designer to recreate the scene in its most authentic state. If you see a performance of the musical *Annie*, it's likely that you'll see a realistic set design. You'll see the ramshackle kitchen at the orphanage where the orphans perform "It's a Hard-Knock Life," with its dirty walls and worn furniture. You'll also see the wealth and splendor of Oliver Warbucks's mansion living room at Christmastime. A realistic set design for *Annie* allows audience members to see for themselves the contrast between the two worlds and feel a greater sense of triumph when the Warbucks mansion ultimately becomes Annie's permanent home.

Theatricalism is another type of set design that is used often in staging performances. The "less is more" style of set design, theatric designs utilize minimal set materials to give more focus to the actors' performances. One of the most famous examples of this type of design is used in Thornton Wilder's *Our Town*, a play-within-a-play in which we are introduced to the hamlet of Grover's Corners through the performance of a stage manager who helps to set the scene. The stage is mostly bare in a production of *Our Town*. In one scene, two actors stand atop ladders to represent two characters talking from the bedroom windows of their homes. Audience members are meant to imagine the scene for themselves. A more modern example is the 2015 revival of *The Color Purple* on Broadway. In the production, actors sit in wooden chairs on a mostly empty stage before a tall, wooden wall affixed with more antique wooden chairs suspended high above. Audience members don't assume that the main character Celie's home has a long, decorative chair wall. They are meant to see and interpret the chairs as the symbol of an important

theme contained within the play: comfort, tradition, motherhood, struggle, or another theme that you as the audience member are meant to infer as you witness the performance.

Other set designers utilize the **expressionist** style of set design. Expressionism doesn't rely on set pieces to accurately set the scene. Instead, audience members are supposed to use what they see on the stage to build to an understanding of an underlying theme. One of the most famous examples of expressionism in the theater can be found in the work of German playwright and director Bertolt Brecht. Brecht famously rejected traditional, realistic theater in favor of dreamlike, nightmarish sets that utilized color and shapes to capture a theme.

Part of a set designer's job is finding which of these types of set design works best with the **source material**. As a set designer, you would work alongside the director and other members of the crew to determine how best to stage a performance.

Set Design in Action

The most important skill required for a set designer is a sense of determination. Set designer Anna Louizos is one of the most in-demand set designers working today. She has designed sets for Broadway's 2013 production of *Cinderella, Avenue Q, High Fidelity, Steel Magnolias, In the Heights, White Christmas,*

The "realistic" set design of *In the Heights* was based on several visits that the set designer made to the New York City neighborhood in which the musical is set: Washington Heights.

and others. For her work on *In the Heights*, Louizos wandered around New York's Washington Heights neighborhood with director Thomas Kail and the show's music composer, Lin-Manuel Miranda (who went on to create the Broadway smash *Hamilton*), to try to capture some of the neighborhood's details. She took lots of photographs and went back to the neighborhood multiple times afterward to study it some more. For Louizos, capturing the grittiness of Washington Heights was key. Said Louizos in an interview with *Playbill*, "When I walk down the street, I notice things. I'm always looking up, I'm always thinking, 'I'm gonna remember *that*.'" *In the Heights* went on to be nominated for a Tony in the set design category.

Set designers must also possess a vast creative sense and a willingness to "think big," often within a strict budget. For Lance Cardinal, who created the set design for a 2011 production of *Little Shop of Horrors* for Callingwood Private School in West Vancouver, British Columbia, a small budget and limited resources was a huge drawback. Cardinal, his partner Jeff, and another friend had to get creative to make the production happen. "We built it all in the school garage and with VERY LITTLE funds. We bought mistinted paint, and asked any friends to help who could," Cardinal said in a post on his blog. The result was a realistic, detailed set that contributed to an amazing performance.

To be a set designer, you also need to possess an ability to work under pressure and deadlines, impeccable people skills, and practical art skills, such as being able to draw or build **models**.

Getting Creative with Set Design

A high school production will likely have a very low set design budget, allowing the opportunity for an amateur set designer to get creative. Talk to your drama instructor about ways you can save money while planning for your high school's next performance. You can often find plenty of student volunteers who want to be involved but tend to shy away from the spotlight and would prefer to help out behind the scenes. If there's a woodworking class at your school, talk to the instructor about recruiting some students from that class who might want to help build sets to help them gain experience. Art students might be willing to help paint sets or source props. Ask around. Talk to your parents or other adults about borrowing any set components or props you might need. Just be sure to keep track of where everything came from so it can be returned later!

Props Mastery 101

The props master might also be referred to as a head of props or props director, but the most commonly used and accepted term is props master. In short, the props master for a theater company is in charge of creating, building, sourcing, organizing, and enacting the use of props for a stage production, in addition to some other duties. According to Chris Beck, head of props for the Eugene O'Neill Theatre, in an interview with *The Producer's Perspective*, it is his job to "load in, assemble, fabricate and handle all props necessary for an attraction at the O'Neill, in addition to maintaining all seats, curtains and furniture owned by the theatre." It's a vast, multifaceted job that requires a lot of creativity, technical know-how, patience, and a positive attitude.

There are different types of props that a props master must be responsible for. The first of these—and what you probably think of when you imagine props in action—are hand props. Hand props are actively used or manipulated by an actor or actors during every performance. A book, a candleholder, or a bag of groceries are all good examples of hand props. Hand props can also fall within the category of **perishable props** that must be replaced every night, such as a piece of cake or fruit that an actor eats onstage, or a letter that gets torn up or destroyed during each performance. Part of a props master's job is determining who will replace the material each time, when it needs to be replaced, and how to budget for that.

The next type of prop for which a props master is responsible is a **set prop**. Set props represent the gray area between the sets department and the props department. If an actor sits down on a couch, that couch is a set prop. The couch is a part of the set, but the actor isn't interacting with it in the same way he might a hand prop. Set props aren't built into the set; nor do they leave stage with an actor at any time. A set designer must be aware of a set prop as he or she designs the rest of the set. Likewise, a props master must keep the set in mind as he or she prepares other props and considers how actors will interact with them. Some other examples of set props include tables, tents, large rocks, and appliances.

Set dressing is another type of prop that also falls partway into the set design department's responsibilities. Set dressing is items that help set a scene, but actors do not actively interact with them. This might include pots and pans in a kitchen or knickknacks on a character's nightstand. Within the category of set dressing, we also have "trim props," which includes curtains and wall hangings, and "practicals," such as lamps, ceiling fans, or chandeliers.

A props master is also responsible for "**greens**," which covers any type of real or artificial flowers, leaves, bushes, trees, or any other type of foliage. A really large tree that requires some special construction will require some help from the set design department.

Any special effects might also be the responsibility of the props department, depending on the size and scope of the effect. These are often done in collaboration with other departments and crews. A campfire bursting to life in a camping scene is the responsibility of the props department. Fog, snow, confetti, or bubbles are referred to as atmospherics and also require planning on the part of the props master and crew, with the help of the electrical crew. **Breakaway props** also fall into the special effects category. Breakaway props are props that are built to break and *will be* broken during a performance. This might include a glass or a bottle, or even a piece of furniture that falls or is thrown during a performance. Breakaway props are tricky because they must break safely without injuring cast, crew, or audience members. And they have to break every time without fail.

Props masters and crews might also be responsible for certain types of sound effects, but this is becoming less common. Before there were sound systems and computers with extensive sound effect libraries, prop crews were responsible for creating any and all sound effects. A roll of thunder could often be attributed to crews shaking a large piece of sheet metal or high impact styrene plastic (called a thunder sheet) backstage. A hand crank–operated wind machine was often used to make the sounds of rushing wind. Props crews were also responsible for any doorbell sounds or phones ringing onstage. In smaller productions on a strict budget, the props department might still be responsible for manually producing sound effects.

The final type of prop is a **personal prop**. Personal props are used by an actor to help develop his or her character. This might include a fan, a pair of glasses, an umbrella, or a cane. Sometimes the inclusion of a personal prop is written into the script. Sometimes an actor will pick it out on his or her own and work it into the performance. Every type of prop mentioned above is important and must be kept organized and performance ready by the props master and crew.

Scope of Responsibilities

In an interview with Eric Hart's *Prop Agenda* website, Tina Stevenson describes one production

Annemieke van Dam, who portrayed Mary Poppins in an Austrian production of the musical, poses with the character's most recognizable prop.

that required a lot of extra effort to get a prop right. The theater was putting on a production of the play *Dinner with Friends*, which involves couples at a table having dinner. So Stevenson needed to make several cakes to be consumed onstage. For this particular production, two of the actresses had food allergies, one to chocolate and the other to oil, which was a huge challenge since the cake needed to at least look like a chocolate cake to the audience, and oil is an important ingredient in cake. Stevenson set to work experimenting with recipes that would keep the actresses safe. She finally made a spice and gingerbread cake made with applesauce and yogurt instead of oil. "The safety of the actress was important to me," said Stevenson. After opening night, one of the actresses confessed that she wasn't actually allergic to oil. She just didn't like eating it.

Other props masters might have to whip up a batch of convincing stage blood, or track down the blueprints of buildings you might see in the early twentieth century in New York, or treat a piece of wood furniture to make it look like an antique. The needs are endless, and a good props master knows that you must be tireless when in pursuit of the perfect prop. "An 'impossibility' goes against my grain," said Tina Stevenson in the same interview with *Prop Agenda*. "I've learned over the years to know when to say 'no, it's not possible.' However, before I say this I exhaust all possibilities. Sometimes 'impossible' doesn't mean there's no way to fabricate or procure an item, but [that] it isn't in the budget, or you don't have the manpower to produce the item."

Organizing Your Props Budget

You're organized and creative, have the tireless spirit of a props master, and are ready to get involved with your high school's next theater production. What can you do to help out, or even take charge? One of the most important things to keep in mind is your budget. Create a spreadsheet listing all of the props you're going to need and how much money you have to spend. Then slowly work your way through the list, almost like a scavenger hunt. Borrow props where you can. Recruit trusted adults to help you build or create other props. Your theater teacher or drama club head can help you get started.

House Carpenter

In 2011, Charlie Rasmussen was the oldest active member of the Local One of the International Alliance of Theatrical Stage Employees. At the age of eighty-five, he was still driving twenty-five minutes a day, six days per week (every day a performance takes place) to New York City's Times Square, the city's theater district, to manage his six-man crew of set workers as head carpenter at the Broadway Theatre. In an interview with *Playbill* he shared his experiences in getting hired early in his career: "An old-timer told me years ago that if I was going to work with my hands, I should go where I'm going to make the most money." Sixty-five years later, he was still going strong with no plans to retire.

If you're the type of person who likes building and creating and working with materials, then

When helping build a set, you'll likely be working with and around a lot of power tools. Stay safe, and be sure to ask a lot of questions before getting to work.

working as the house carpenter of a theater might be for you. Of course, at a high school level, the heavier carpentry and use of power tools will probably be handled by an adult. However, working alongside a more experienced carpenter gives you the perfect opportunity to learn and ask questions, and to build your skills.

A theater's house carpenter must work with the set designer, props master, and crew to build sometimes simple, sometimes more elaborate pieces to be used onstage.

A strong background in carpentry is the most important skill required for a set builder. One flaw can cause a set to come crashing down, so it's important to hone your skills. In 2005, opera singer David Rendall shattered his hip and knee and injured his shoulders when a set collapsed on him during a performance of *Aida* at the Royal Danish Theater in Copenhagen. Safety is a top priority for a carpenter, so it's important to learn and ask questions and communicate well with the rest of your crew.

Everyone who works in props and sets as part of a theater production has a large list of responsibilities. Performing those responsibilities in an organized and careful manner is the result of a great deal of planning, leadership, and, most importantly, teamwork.

One of the most rewarding parts of theater work is research. What works within a certain time period and what doesn't? The library will have the answer.

CHAPTER THREE
PERFORMANCE READY

Y ou did it! You signed up to participate in a theater production, either as a leader of a crew or as a crewmember. The acting roles have been cast. Now it's time to think about your specific tasks and how you will accomplish each one over the course of the next several weeks, as you go from the planning period for the first performance, through opening night, to the moment the curtain has closed on the final performance, and afterward. For the props and sets crews, the next few weeks are crucial to planning every detail.

At the earliest stages, regardless of whether you are working on set design or props, your first task is simply sitting down with the script and reading it—as many times as necessary. Your crew will then have to formulate a plan. Does the entire play take place in a single setting? How often does the setting change? Where should the door be placed so that when Character A enters in the second act, the entire audience can see him? What kind of lamp should be used in the first act in order to convey the time period and that the characters are caught up in a financial struggle? Details are extremely important at this stage. A good set designer or props master must take copious notes on the script, whether the notes are kept electronically or in a notebook. (You can also write notes in the margins of your copy of the play, as long as it belongs to you and not your school or library.) Those notes will continue to play a role until the final curtain on the final performance. Also, they might serve as inspiration for the next production in which you take part, so keep all of your ideas on file for easy reference.

Planning Props and Set Design

After you've had a chance to read over the script carefully and take notes, you'll want to take a look at what you have to work with. If you're unfamiliar with the stage the cast and crew will be using, walk out onto it and try to get a feel for the theater. There are several types of theaters, which we'll examine below. You might want to go out into the seats and sit in the farthest row from the stage. What's visible from where you're sitting? Take a camera or smartphone along and snap photos so that you can keep the **point of view** of every audience member in mind as you begin to plan. Is the theater small and cozy? Or is it large and austere? How does being in the theater itself make you feel? How do you want it to make you feel? What can you do, in helping to plan the performance, to bring the emotion you want to convey to the excited audience member sitting in the very front row *and* to the person sitting in the very last row of the balcony?

One important aspect that a set designer and props master—and the crewmembers they work with—must take into consideration is the stage you have to work with. There are different types of stages, and that affects how you ultimately plan the performance. The stage will have a profound affect on what kind of sets you can use, how you can change the sets and props, where the sets and props will be stored when not in use, and whether you can set up one set behind a curtain while the actors continue the play in front of the curtain. Let's look at some of the different types of stages you might encounter.

Proscenium Stage

If you attend a lot of theater performances, you've encountered a proscenium stage. This is the most common type. A proscenium stage essentially places a performance within a "frame" for the audience. There are wings on either side of the stage, outside of the audience's view, and a backstage area. When planning

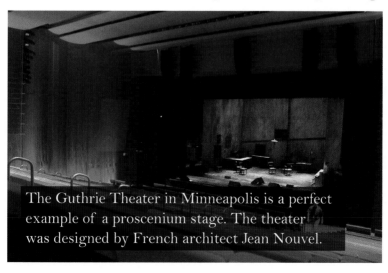

The Guthrie Theater in Minneapolis is a perfect example of a proscenium stage. The theater was designed by French architect Jean Nouvel.

a performance on a proscenium stage, you must take what's visible to the audience into consideration at all times. You have to work within the frame.

Thrust Stage

A thrust stage extends out so that the audience sits on three sides of it. Shakespeare's Globe Theatre employed a type of thrust stage. A thrust stage can help to bring the performance closer to the audience, creating a sense of intimacy between the audience and performers. On a thrust stage, sets and props must be created and placed with the audience's ability to see the performers in mind. You likely wouldn't use a large, bulky set on a thrust stage because it would block the audience's view on at least one side of the stage.

An end stage is a type of thrust stage that extends from a wall, but the audience sits only on one side and not around it. There are usually neither wings nor curtains to hide any of the action.

Arena Theater

In an arena theater, the audience sits around the stage on all sides, and the performance takes place in the middle. The stage is often a raised platform so that the audience can see the action. This is the case in the 2015–2016 Broadway production of *Fun Home*, which helps to convey a sense of unity and warmth with the audience by allowing them to witness the action from any side of the stage. As with a thrust theater, all props and sets must be placed with the audience's sight line in mind.

Black Box Theater

A black box theater or flexible theater is one that is essentially a black box in which nothing is fixed in place. This includes the seating, the lighting, any sets used, etc. The idea behind a black box theater is that it creates a neutral environment that can be open to the director's/actors'/set designer's interpretation. A black box theater can allow for the audience to sit on one side (as with a proscenium theater), three sides (as with a thrust theater), four sides (as in an arena theater), or even allow the play's action to take place within the audience.

Creating Your Vision

Once you've sized up the stage itself, you will have to talk to the director to get his or her vision for the show. Put that in your notes to keep as a reference. According to Harvard's *Student Technical Theatre Handbook*, you'll want to "Make sure you read the play at least twice before sitting down to design. You want to pick out what set design/large prop things that the script calls for as well as getting a feel for the **arc**, mood, and themes of the play. Don't just settle for the director's summary. The better you know the play, the better you can question the director on his/her choices, influences, and needs." What you envision for a performance might be quite different from what the director and actors might expect. So it's important to make a plan and be able to share your vision effectively. If you enjoy building models, do that. If you enjoy sketching, draw your sets or the backdrops that will be painted.

Present your design/plan in the way you think it will be the most effective. And be prepared to fight for your vision, but be flexible and open minded. You want the director and crew to be on your side. Props master, be ready with a list of the props the production will need, which ones you'll be making, which you'll be sourcing, and what your plan is for accomplishing that. The set designer and props master will also meet with each other frequently to come up with a collaborative vision for the performance. Who will create/find the wall sconces for the living room set, and who will mount them?

The role of the stage manager is one whose importance cannot be stressed enough. A stage manager is exactly that: a manager. Therefore, you will have to communicate with this person during all stages of planning and performing the play. Stage managers provide support to the cast and crew throughout the course of a production. They are also in charge of making sure that every performance runs smoothly. In a small community or high school production, the director might also act as stage manager.

The stage manager is responsible for:

- Scheduling and running rehearsals

- Communicating the director's wishes to cast and crew

- Calling actor cues during a performance

- Marking out the set dimensions on the stage floor

- Overseeing every performance, from beginning to end

The stage manager is the keeper of the "master copy" of the script, called the prompt book. Every set change, every cue, every delivery of every prop is kept in the prompt book, and it's the stage manager's job to make sure that every task, both onstage and off, is performed at precisely the right moment.

The director or the stage manager will present a rehearsal schedule along with a list of dates by which certain props and sets will be required. It will be up to the crews to create a build schedule so everything is ready when it is needed. At this point, crewmembers will receive any special training they need to build a set or make a prop. Also, crewmembers will be given a work schedule so they can be present when their projects are being made. It is crucial that people honor this schedule because the crews are interdependent. Painters can't do their work until sets are finished, and their paint must be dry before any actors touch the sets.

Some actors will need some props if they are to rehearse a scene correctly. If a prop is not completed on time, it can ruin an actor's preparation. So, if something must be built, someone should be assigned to start on it right away.

After meeting with the director and other pertinent heads of crew, go back to your notes. How does your meeting with the director change your vision? Rework what you need to, keeping the director's notes in mind. Once you're happy with your work, bring it back to the table for a second look.

And remember (this is very important), feedback is not criticism. If you're asked to rework your plan or design it a second, or even a third or fourth, time, it's OK. Keep an open mind and be willing to listen; this will help to create a good relationship between you and the director. Harmony within the cast and crew makes for a happier production.

You should also be prepared to talk budget. Are you working with a few hundred dollars or a few thousand? How many crewmembers will be at the ready to help you bring your vision to life? You might want to create a budgeting spreadsheet at this stage to share with the director and crew. How much money do you have allocated for building the set? How much

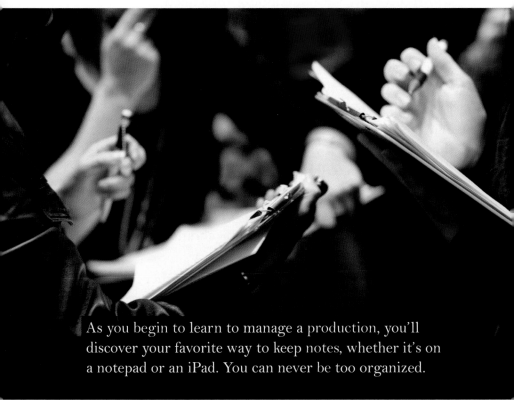

As you begin to learn to manage a production, you'll discover your favorite way to keep notes, whether it's on a notepad or an iPad. You can never be too organized.

can you spend on a particular prop? If you have $500 to spend and use $250 to buy a chair that is perfect for the show's time period, you've spent half your budget on a single prop. Would a less expensive chair change the audience's experience? These are questions you have to ask yourself as you begin to plan your budget.

Managing a Crew

You've got the list of props and sets needed. You've got the build schedule set. You've got the budget. Now what? At this point, you might want to sit down with your crew, share your plan, and establish a good working relationship with them. At the high school level, everyone is volunteering their time, and many are also trying to balance a full schedule of schoolwork and other after-school activities. On the first day, find out when everyone is available so you can establish a realistic work schedule. Program everyone's cell phone number into your phone so you can send out a text an hour before work starts. And create incentives. Can you use part of the budget to order pizza for your crew after a hard day of work?

Crew is a very general term used for the people who work within a specific department on a theater production. You might be a part of the props crew, responsible—under the props master's direction— for finding, creating, storing, and organizing the different props components. The set crew, under the guidance of the set designer and head carpenter, work to build, find, and create different set components. During a performance, a crewmember is responsible for moving, storing, and organizing different set and

Set construction is under way on this stage in Berlin, Germany. The set crew, props department, lighting, and sound must coordinate everything in order for the production to go off without a hitch.

props components. After a performance, a crewmember might have to replace a prop before the next performance, organize, and do a quick inventory to make sure that all props have been put away. A set crewmember might have to make repairs, touch up a piece of the set, and just make sure that everything is in working order before the next performance. There are people designated as runners who move sets or props so they are in the right place at the right time. Runners should have scripts on which they mark their cues so they can do their jobs in a timely manner.

Theater productions also require assistants who work alongside a set designer or props master, but not necessarily as part of the crew. Assistants might work to set and organize meetings with other members of the production. They might answer phones and take messages. They might take and keep notes. Assistants manage the administrative responsibilities that are inevitably part of the day-to-day work.

You might be leading crewmembers who have worked on plays previously, or you might be working with student novices who need a lot of guidance and support. It's important to treat everyone with a high level of respect. And ask lots of questions! Just because you're in charge of the crew doesn't necessarily mean that you know everything there is to know. An older crewmember might have some ideas that you haven't heard before. A younger, less experienced crewmember might have experience in areas with which you are unfamiliar. A crew novice might be an expert at sewing or papier-mâché. So ask questions and listen to the answers. If you are one of those novices with some expertise, speak up and let someone know what you can do.

The first meeting with the crew is your opportunity to share your vision for the production and delegate tasks to your crewmembers. At this point, you should know every detail of your plan and how it will play out over the course of the performance. Which crewmember will hand the basket to the actor playing Character A in the second act? When that prop isn't needed onstage, who will be in charge of storing and keeping track of it—the actor or a crewmember? Where will the props be stored? All props should have a place they are kept when not in use. Some props masters have props

As a member of the props department, part of your job is to keep tabs on any props and make sure they are at the ready for the next performance.

lockers where items are stored. If there is room offstage, a props table can be set up with a place designated for each prop. An outline of the prop should be drawn so it is easy to see which one goes where—tool kits or carpentry shops are often organized this way. By outlining a prop, it is easy for everyone to see when something is missing.

One trick in set design is to create platforms on wheels that have sets on multiple sides. These allow for quick scene changes with a spin of the platform. Which crewmembers or actors will rotate the set after a street scene to set the stage for the living room scene? If done efficiently, the scene change can enhance the performance and draw enthusiastic applause. These should all be part of your plan. Talk your crewmembers through the plan. Answer questions. Your goal is to get your crew organized and motivated at this stage.

Building Your Vision

Now that your crew is on board, it's time to get started with creating. Be prepared to get your hands dirty! The set designer and props master should be as handy with a drill or a paintbrush as any other member of the crew. It's common in high school theater for crewmembers to wear many hats.

In the early part of production, the crew and the cast will not spend much time together. Their work schedules may not even overlap. Rehearsals may be after dinner, but production work may start right after school. If you're the set designer working with a student crew, as you would in a high school production, take a quick roll call to make sure everyone on your work schedule is present.

Someone on the crew should be in charge of research; he or she sets the standards for historical accuracy. The set designer needs to ensure those standards are kept. That person also needs to monitor projects so that they don't get off track. All work must conform to the vision of the play.

The set designer also needs to meet with the director and the person in charge of lighting to learn the lighting plan for each scene. Lighting will affect the look of sets and backdrops. It's important that paint colors are selected by how they will look to the audience and not how they will look in the workshop.

Once something is built, you'll want to test it and test it again to make sure that it's not going to fail during a performance or detract from the action onstage. Your props must be foolproof and your sets must be top notch, down to the smallest caster wheel. During the creation stage, it's important to communicate your needs with your crew and to keep the director informed. Sometimes things go wrong. Maybe that ladder you borrowed to use in your production of *Our Town* is wobbly. Perhaps a measurement is wrong and a piece of the set has to be rebuilt. It's up to you to convey to your crew what needs to be fixed and to provide a timeline. No one likes to have to redo work that he or she has already spent a great deal of time on, so be sure to play your role diplomatically. And remember that the earlier you catch a problem, the faster it can be fixed.

Building and maintaining a set requires precision, patience, and the highest level of quality control. Things can break and need to be fixed quickly.

ERIC HART'S AGENDA

Eric Hart started out like a lot of props masters: in his high school theater department. Nowadays, he's a successful freelance props master with clients such as the Public Theater, the Santa Fe Opera, the Ethel Barrymore Theatre, and even Macy's, Saks Fifth Avenue, and Lord & Taylor. He often talks about his work in his blog, *Prop Agenda*.

In an interview with About.com, Hart talks about his favorite part of the job: "I like that on any given day, I am dealing with all parts of my brain as well as working with my hands. I can be thinking about history, characters, science, chemistry, art or design; sometimes all at once."

In order to prepare for his career, Eric Hart took shop classes in junior high and in high school, and then majored in theater in college. His parents, both potters, introduced him to sculpting and carving, both skills that came into play later on in his career. But other skills that he learned have benefited him as well. Hart says in the same interview that he's glad he took AP English in high school because it has helped him to communicate well with his coworkers. "Every once in awhile," he writes, "I've seen someone send an e-mail that is so poorly written, you don't even know what they are trying to say or what point they're making."

The job comes with challenges. The director might want a special change made to a prop that isn't

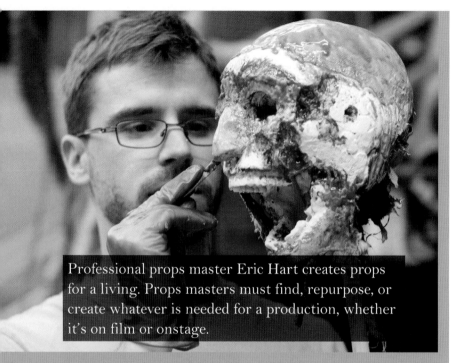

Professional props master Eric Hart creates props for a living. Props masters must find, repurpose, or create whatever is needed for a production, whether it's on film or onstage.

physically possible, or he or she might want it within an impossible time frame. This is when Hart has to do his best to fulfill a need, but within reason, and tell a director when something is impossible. Part of being a props master is to work things out with the director so that everyone is happy with the result. Says Hart, "It's not a props person's place to be at odds with the director or designer. Usually, if a situation begins to arise, it's because someone is requesting something which is physically impossible. If that's the case, I will make a few suggestions, each with a different kind of compromise."

Time for Rehearsal

The rehearsal phase of the production is when you can finally put your hard work to the test. Arrive on time for rehearsals and be prepared to stay for the entire time. As part of a team, you want to show that you're working as hard as the other crewmembers and cast.

In theater, there are a few different types of rehearsals, which go on for an average of five to six weeks. Let's take a brief look at them.

Read-Throughs

A read-through is the rehearsal that takes place once the show is cast. The cast and crew gathers together to meet and go over the script. Often, the cast members sit around a table and simply read the entire script out loud as they begin to get a feel

Actors rehearse for a performance onstage in Moscow. Understanding how to use a prop safely and well is as much a part of an actor's job as learning her lines!

for their individual parts. The director might provide some notes at this stage. As set designer or props master, while you won't play an active role in a read-through, this is your chance to reread the script and familiarize yourself with the individual actor cues. An actor saying, "Good night!" followed by a blackout might be your cue to move a particular prop or set. So it's good to start committing your cues to memory as soon as possible.

Blocking Rehearsals

A blocking rehearsal takes place with the characters onstage, in position, as they perform particular scenes that the director would like to work through. This gives the director the chance to finalize "blocking" and ensure that everything is running smoothly. Blocking is the setup of the precise position and movement of the actors throughout the performance. This is your chance to see how the actors begin to interact with the sets and utilize the props. Say an actor picks up the handset of an antique phone that you found at a thrift store in the third act and the phone's cord comes loose. During a performance, a mistake like that will immediately take the audience out of the scene. It's your job to find a way to fix the phone so that the actor can do his or her job. Or perhaps an actor's entrance through a door in the set is interrupted because the door squeaks or sticks or falls open again once it's closed. After seeing this happen during a general rehearsal, you can add fixing the door to your to-do list before the next rehearsal.

Polishing Rehearsals

Polishing rehearsals allow the director to run through particular scenes in order to "polish" the performance. Sometimes a director may spend an entire rehearsal working through one scene again and again until everything is running smoothly. The next rehearsal, he or she might do the same with a different scene. At the polishing rehearsal stage, all props and sets should be in excellent working order. This is your chance to work out any final kinks.

Technical Rehearsal

The technical rehearsal is a run-through of the entire performance from beginning to end. But instead of paying close attention to the actors, the director will instead be focused on perfecting the timing of the lights and sound and any other technical issue that comes up. There might be pauses in the middle of an act so that the director (or stage manager) and head of lighting can discuss a missed cue or a malfunctioning piece of lighting equipment. This is the final rehearsal before the dress rehearsal. Once the technical rehearsal is over, cast and crew should be able to get through an entire performance without any problems.

Dress Rehearsal

The dress rehearsal is the final rehearsal before the first performance. The cast and crew run through the entire play or musical, uninterrupted, as if this is the first performance. The director will only sit and watch and deliver any notes at the end. This is your chance to do the same and make any fixes before the first performance. You might have some late-breaking ideas now that you're seeing your vision in action. So might the director. A stage production is a work in progress up until the first performance, and sometimes beyond. Keep notes and be prepared to share them with the director, head of lighting, costume designer, and others. Rehearsals are for everyone, not just the actors on the stage. This can also be a fun time for the cast and the crew. Both groups have been working long hours to make the show happen, and this is the time each group gets to see the results of the other's labor. When costumes, sets, props, lighting, and sound come together for the first time, it can be exhilarating for everyone.

Performance Time

You've come a long way since someone first placed the script in your hands. The big day has arrived. Everyone is buzzing with that nervous excitement that seems to only exist in a theater. You're about to embark on the first performance.

You'll want to arrive at the theater extra early on the day of the first performance. That will give you time to check over everything and make sure it's in place. If you're the props master, check in with the individual members of your crew. Is everyone there? Are they all feeling prepared? Hold a quick meeting and go through your notes with your entire crew present. Run through the list of props and make sure that every prop is in place. If actors carry specific personal props,

Before a performance begins, any and all props have to be organized and ready to go. After each performance, every prop must find its way back to where it can be ready to go again.

make sure they have them and that the props, and any possible backup props, are in working order.

The head of set design and the carpenters will want to get together and check out the entire set and make sure that everything is in working order. If something seems faulty, make sure it's checked out as soon as possible. Meet with your crew and run through any outstanding issues.

As a member of the crew, you'll want to speak to your department head or team leader to find out if there are any last-minute tasks that need to be taken care of. And then don't hesitate to get them done. The most important task on opening night is to communicate with the other members of the crew and with the cast.

Once the audience begins to arrive, any work on the stage must be already completed, so be ready to plan accordingly. To communicate with members of your crew, you'll need to speak quietly. Theaters are designed to project sound outward. Sometimes even noise coming from the "back of house" can cause a distraction. You want audience members to never lose the illusion that the onstage action is real.

Curtain Up!

You've checked and double-checked everything in your notes. The stage manager gives the word. The performance is about to begin. From backstage, you'll need to be ready for anything to go wrong, and if it does, be prepared to leap into action. During opening night, you might even want to keep your copy of the script on hand to keep an eye on cues. Is everything running smoothly? If not, ask yourself if there is something you can do to fix the issue.

All members of the crew must concentrate completely during the performance. Don't be tempted to watch the play. The time for that was during dress rehearsal. If you get caught watching, you might miss a cue, which could make an actor miss theirs. You must always stay out of view; if you can see the audience, the audience can see you. And make sure you don't get in the way of actors entering and exiting or of runners changing scenery. If you are a runner, you should make sure you wear your black outfit so you are as invisible as possible.

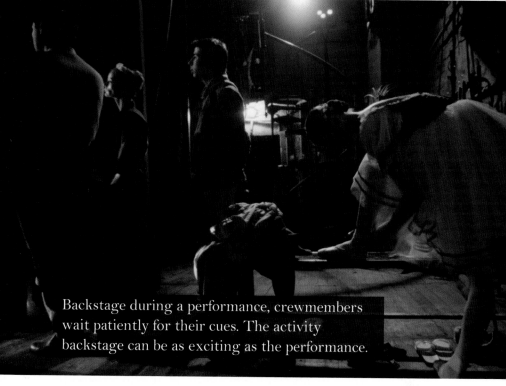

Backstage during a performance, crewmembers wait patiently for their cues. The activity backstage can be as exciting as the performance.

After the Performance

The performance is over, and the cast is taking their bows. All in all, it was an excellent show. You should feel proud. You should congratulate the cast on a great performance as they leave the stage. This is a moment of celebration for everyone involved in the performance. To stage a performance is a huge undertaking, and for it to go off without a hitch is a sign that you and the other members of cast and crew worked well together.

Now that the performance is over, the cast might be able to go right home or out to dinner to celebrate a job well done, but as a crewmember, your night is only just beginning. As props master, go through your preperformance list and make sure that everything is back in its place, all ready for the next performance. As set designer or a member of the set crew, you'll want to address any issues with the set itself. The set has to be maintained. Once you feel comfortable and happy with a job well done, it's time to go out and celebrate, even if that means going home and getting a good night's rest before the next performance.

Closing Night and Beyond

Now we come to the most bittersweet part of a production … closing night. You've had a great run. Every performance was stellar and was rewarded with a standing ovation. You're still flying high on adrenaline, and that feels good. But all good things must come to an end, and that is particularly true in theater. The cast and crew cannot continue working indefinitely, and eventually even the greatest productions close. So what now?

If you've managed a crew over the course of the production, thank each and every person with whom you worked. You might even want to get your crewmembers a little closing night gift. Congratulate the cast and the director, and just let everyone know that you had a great time and would love to work with all of them again in the future. Who knows? The director might even be so touched that he or she will want you on his or her next production. There will likely be a closing night party, and you should go and have a good time and not think about the massive cleanup and dismantling of the set you and the other members of crew will have to perform very soon.

Striking the Set

Once you've had a chance to celebrate, it's time to start preparing the theater for the next production. In order for the theater to be prepared for something new, you and the other members of the crew have to tear down the set. The props room must be reorganized and things must be put away neatly in case they can be reused. It's a massive undertaking, but as long as you continue to be as organized as you were during the production's earlier stages, it should run smoothly.

As head of a crew, you should be prepared to delegate tasks. Who will actually disassemble the set, and where will the pieces of the set be stored? This is something to discuss with the head carpenter and set crew. Painted backdrops might be rolled up and stored for use in future productions. Large set prop items, such as chairs and other furniture, will need to be returned, if they were borrowed, or placed in a designated storage place. Some theaters might sell off unneeded furniture in order to help finance the next production. As head of props, that job might fall into your list of tasks, so check with the theater's general manager in order to make an effective plan. Items that can be reused should be stored somewhere they will remain undamaged. The props room should be returned to a clean and organized state so that important items can easily be located for the next production. Clean up any sawdust or dirt that gathered during the set teardown.

Disassembling a set is thirsty work, so frequently check in with members of your crew to make sure they're drinking plenty of water. You might want to provide healthy snacks to help your crew keep up their strength. Once the set is torn down, everything has been organized, and the theater has been tidied, your part in the production is done. Now you can prepare for your next big production!

After the last performance of a production, the crewmembers begin the slow process of dismantling the set, cleaning up, and organizing all hardware and supplies.

British actress of stage and screen Celia Imrie portrays Dotty Otley in this 2012 production of *Noises Off*, a play based around the idea of a production going completely off the rails.

CHAPTER FOUR

WHEN THINGS FALL APART

If you are familiar with the play *Noises Off,* you probably already know all about all of the things that can go wrong during a performance. In a performance of *Noises Off,* you have the opportunity to see the first act of a play both from the house (audience's perspective) and backstage. Doors slam, actors miss their cues and mess up their lines, and there are continuous mishaps involving a plate of sardines. In short, nothing is going right. The idea of theater mishaps is so famous, playwright Michael Frayn wrote a whole play about it!

But as they say in theater, "The show must go on!" and often that means overcoming incredible odds. Anything that can go wrong often does, even with the utmost levels of planning and organization. A crewmember might make a misstep. A part of the set might break. A piece of equipment used for a special effect might malfunction, ruining the moment for the audience. Or an injury might occur. And when something like this happens, you might be the one who needs to correct the issue. That requires quick thinking and the ability to handle extreme stress under pressure.

Here is one example from the Rockville Musical Theater, which keeps an updated list of mishaps on its website. The props master for *Sweet Charity* forgot to put out a wedding gift. The actor who was to present the gift was resourceful enough to go offstage and get it himself.

A Minor Mishap

If a mishap is going to occur during a performance, you would hope it is something minor, especially if the mistake was your fault or the fault of one of your crewmembers.

On the Roundabout Theatre Company blog, cast and crew members shared some of their experiences with shows that didn't exactly go as planned. According to Roundabout apprentice Sari Stifelman, she once saw a performance of *Legally Blonde* on Broadway during which the actress playing Elle Woods did the "bend and snap" so hard during one iconic scene that her wig came off. Another story told the legendary tale of an actor playing Othello who wasn't presented with the prop dagger the character used during his suicide scene. Without a weapon, the actor could only improvise and "break" his own neck.

Says Elizabeth Kandel, Roundabout's associate director of marketing, "I saw *Dracula, the Musical* on Broadway, on what proved to be a bad night, technically speaking. First, a door that came up from the stage didn't close properly into the door frame, so it couldn't go back into the stage the way it came up. A man with a headset had to come out and hammer the door frame—IN THE MIDDLE OF A SONG—

to get it to close and go back into the floor. If that weren't enough, a few scenes later a coffin wheeled out on stage. Nothing happened. Still nothing happened. Finally, our friend with the headset came out, hammered on the back of the coffin, and suddenly the coffin opened and out popped Tom Hewitt (the actor playing Dracula). If you ask me, the man in the headset should have gotten to take a bow at that performance."

After each of these events occurred, cast and crew worked together to keep the performance on track. Often, as with the case of the *Othello* actor and his missing dagger, you can rely on the cast to "cover" for a mistake without breaking character. Other times, as in the case of the performance of *Dracula* gone awry, a member of the crew had to step in and take care of the issue (or issues) as quickly as possible. If a minor mishap occurs and an immediate fix does not present itself, as in the case of the *Legally Blond* wig mishap, your point person is the stage manager. A production's stage manager is in charge during a performance. He or she will know how to fix the mistake and the right time at which to fix it.

Everyone Makes Mistakes

This point cannot be stressed enough: everyone makes mistakes. Even the most experienced, most professional member of the crew will make a mistake on occasion. Some of those mistakes might be caught just in time. Some of them might be disastrous. The key is for crewmembers to never lose their concentration and to not panic when something does go wrong.

Actress Mary Martin "flies" during a rehearsal of *Peter Pan*. This production opened in 1954 and ran for 152 performances.

In 1960, famed Broadway actress Mary Martin was teaching her young *Peter Pan* costars how to fly during a rehearsal. A series of cables manned by crewmembers were used to create the illusion. However, a new crewmember became so mesmerized by the magic of the moment, he forgot that he was supposed to pull Martin away from the wall, mid-flight. The actress hit the wall and broke her elbow in two places. Ever the professional, she went back to her mark and prepared for her cue because she didn't want her young costars to be afraid to fly. The next day, there was a mattress affixed high on the wall with a sign that read "MARY MARTIN CRASHED HERE." In that situation, a crewmember made a mistake, and it resulted in an injury. Other disasters have occurred due to a technical malfunction.

A few performances before her final appearance as Elphaba in *Wicked*, Idina Menzel took a misstep through the trapdoor that was used for the melting sequence and fell several feet below the stage, bruising several ribs. Broadway productions can gross millions of dollars (several have topped $1 billion), so completely stopping the performance and refunding theatergoers thousands of dollars was out of the question. The show had to go on. The curtains were closed to help preserve the moment for the audience as crewmembers rushed to get Idina Menzel's understudy into costume and makeup. After a forty-five-minute delay, the curtains opened on a brand-new Elphaba, and Menzel spent the rest of the evening in the hospital. The mishap was later traced to a malfunction in the computer program that lowered the trapdoor. The malfunction caused the trapdoor to lower before the actress was standing on it. Members of the crew worked to fix the malfunction, and in March 2016, *Wicked* broke $1 billion in box office sales—the fastest a Broadway production had ever met that goal.

What can you do to prevent mistakes like these? Sometimes you can't do anything. However, you can work hard to prepare for every possible mishap. As set designer, you'll want to plan the set design carefully in order to prevent accidents. Communicate with the director and other members of the crew about potential safety hazards. Test and test again every moving part of the set to make sure that it is in good working order before every performance. A props master will want to secure props in place, using glue, tape, or nails as necessary. For breakables or props that are consumed over the course of the performance, always have a few backups on hand in case something accidentally gets broken. Store backups in a convenient location and let everyone know how to access them. Check breakable props for jagged edges that might cut any actor using them. As a member of the crew, report any potential dangers to your immediate supervisor. As they say, "If you see something, say something."

Close Call

The musical *Sweeney Todd: The Demon Barber of Fleet Street* is a tale of a murderous barber who slits the throats of those who have wronged him in the past—and anyone else who gets in his way. It has been a favorite of audiences for almost forty years, but

THE CURSE OF THE SCOTTISH PLAY

Perhaps you have heard someone say, "Break a leg!" before a performance. There is a perfectly good explanation for that, and it's good, old superstition. It's believed that saying, "Good luck" to a performer before a show will only cause things to go wrong, so by saying, "Break a leg!" you're hoping the opposite will happen. Superstition around the theater has been going on for centuries.

One of the most popular cases of superstition in the theater involves the play *Macbeth*. It is believed that uttering the name "Macbeth" within the confines of the theater will bring misfortune down upon cast and crew, so you must refer to one of Shakespeare's greatest works as "The Scottish Play" or "The Bard's Play."

The play's superstitious history allegedly began during one of its earliest performances, when the actor slated to play Lady Macbeth died suddenly. In the seventeenth century, an actor playing King Duncan was killed after a fake dagger was replaced by a real one. In 1947, the actor playing Macbeth himself was killed onstage when a stage fight got out of hand. Stories relating to the curse of the Scottish Play go back centuries.

So, what should you do if you accidentally utter the word "Macbeth"? Quickly exit the theater, spin around three times, spit over your left shoulder, and recite a line from Shakespeare.

Actors portray the ill-fated titular role and Judge Turpin in this Welsh production of *Sweeney Todd*. The razor blade prop used here is fake, and special effects are used to make it seem real.

for two student actors in New Zealand in 2016, the performance got a little too real.

The razor blade prop wielded by the show's main character was a real razor blade. The props master had taken special care to dull the blade and cover it with duct tape so that no one would be injured. But the edge was still extremely sharp, and during the performance, the blade inflicted serious injury to the throats of two of the actors. Both actors were hospitalized and lived through the ordeal without permanent harm.

This brings up a key consideration for set designers and props masters for high school shows. The actors in those shows aren't trained to handle scenes such as the ones in *Sweeney Todd*. In professional theater, weapons used are real. Swords and knives may be dulled, but they still are dangerous. However, the actors are trained in stage combat; they must prove proficiency to get certified for different levels of stage combat. Students won't have that proficiency, so props should be chosen for safety.

Stories of injury due to a prop malfunction or set collapse are all too common. So what should you do if an injury occurs during a rehearsal or a performance of which you are a part? In the case of an injury involving cast or crew, if you are the first person on the scene and have witnessed the injury, you must take action. Call 911 or direct another member of the crew to do so while you aid the injured party. Send another member of the crew to let the stage manager know that an injury has occurred, if he or she isn't already aware. The top priority at this moment is no longer the show, but the health and welfare of the injured person. The stage manager will make an announcement to the audience, letting them know the situation, and will determine whether or not the show will continue and under what means. As during a performance, the cast and crew must work together to get help while maintaining a safe environment in which everyone is communicating effectively.

THE PROBLEM WITH PROP WEAPONS

Prop weapons can be very, very dangerous when not handled with extreme care. They have been used in performances for centuries and are often accompanied by stories of accidental injury. A props master's most important job is to guarantee the safety of actors and crew. Therefore, if you are participating in a performance that requires a prop weapon, be sure to follow these safety guidelines.

Treat prop weapons as if they are real weapons. Insist that members of the cast and crew do the same. Create a list of guidelines to be posted in a clearly visible location, outlining the rules for handling a prop weapon. Don't be afraid to enforce your rules.

Insist that every prop weapon, no matter how harmless it seems, be thoroughly examined and have any sharp points or edges filed down.

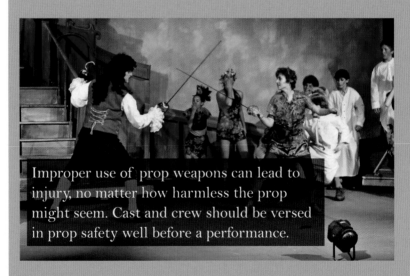

Improper use of prop weapons can lead to injury, no matter how harmless the prop might seem. Cast and crew should be versed in prop safety well before a performance.

Keep edged weapons, such as swords or daggers, even if they are made from plastic or plywood, in a specific location and count them after every performance to ensure that all are there. Keep a bin just offstage and ask actors to place any weapons in the bin when they aren't in use. Assign specific weapons to specific actors in order to keep track of who is using which weapon. That way, when something goes missing, you'll know with whom to speak.

Examine every prop weapon before every performance to ensure that none have been broken, damaged, or tampered with. A broken or damaged stage weapon can lead to a very real injury.

Do not allow anyone to play with any props outside of their intended use. Props should be used only during rehearsal or performance.

Look for alternatives to a weapon. You will likely not encounter a prop firearm during a high school performance. But in college and on the professional stage, prop firearms might be used, and they are extremely dangerous. Most times, prop firearms have been altered so they can be used only with blanks. However, they can still cause harm. If possible, discuss alternatives with the director. Is a prop firearm 100 percent necessary? Can the production integrate the use of pantomime and special effects instead?

Stand by your principles. The safety of the cast and crew is more important than someone's hurt feelings.

Outside Factors

Sometimes the issue will have nothing to do at all with the performance and everything to do with outside factors, such as inclement weather or fire. The most important thing to remember in one of these situations is not to panic. It's important to keep a cool head and trust that everyone around you will do the same. Assess the situation. Are people in danger? The production's stage manager is your point person for handling an emergency like this, as he or she knows the emergency procedure and will be the one to determine whether the performance will end or continue. If danger is imminent, he or she will make an announcement, directing cast, crew, and audience members to safety. Follow the stage manager's instructions, being sure to help those around you to understand the situation and make their way to safety.

Another outside factor that might cause delays to the performance is "audience interruption." In July 2015, right before a performance of *Hand to God* on Broadway, an audience member jumped onstage to use a nonworking electrical outlet that was part of the set to charge his cell phone. The preperformance music was immediately stopped, and the crew removed the phone and then made an announcement, warning audience members not to climb onstage or interfere with the set in any way. Had no one noticed, the phone and charger could have caused damage to the set and delayed the performance.

Arguments and Fighting

One of the biggest drawbacks to performing on a theater crew is the time commitment. The work is done after school, sometimes late in the evening. This can play havoc with study and sleep schedules. In some cases, people miss deadlines and create an emergency for other crewmembers. In this common scenario, the days leading up to the show can be very long. After all, a set must be completed for the show to go on. Crewmembers can get very grumpy.

In a theater with a lot of people under pressure to do well, disagreements are bound to occur. Arguments can be extremely distracting and might even disrupt a performance if they get out of hand. And if you are managing a crew, it's your job to intervene when necessary. You yourself might find that you are involved in a disagreement with a member of the cast or crew. It's important during these events to keep a cool head and not let the disagreement interfere with any rehearsal or performance. Plan a time to discuss a disagreement once you've had time to calm down and think rationally. You might even want to invite another person in to act as an objective third party and help you resolve the issue.

Disagreements among cast and crew happen, but keeping the production on track is of the utmost importance. Someone of authority should intervene as soon as possible.

The skills you learn in the theater can be applied to almost any career field you enter into later on in life. A costume designer may go on to design her own line of clothing.

CHAPTER FIVE
ENTERING THE WORLD STAGE

I f you have caught the theater bug, there are opportunities for staying involved in theater after your high school drama experience ends. There are careers out there, both in theater and outside of theater, which will allow you to apply the skills you've learned. You can continue onward to a career as a set designer or props master for a large theater company. Or you might choose to build furniture for a living or manage a team as the owner of your own baking business. The skills you take with you are ones that you'll have for life. So let's take a look at some things you can do with your newly honed theater skills.

Working in Theater

You've thought about it a lot, and you want to continue down the path toward a career as a professional set designer, props master, or other related job. The good news is that you don't need to get a formal education to do that. Most theater stagehands will tell you that the best education is hands-on training inside a working theater in an entry-level role. What better way to gain experience than under the stage lights, or backstage on opening night? However, a lot of theater professionals recommend taking classes or even getting a degree in a related field such as art or design if you want to improve your chances of finding a solid job. Most props masters have at least an associate's degree. So even if you feel like you're ready to jump right in, it can't hurt to take a few classes or talk to a guidance counselor or college advisor about what majors and colleges would work best for you. To get an edge on the competition—and there will be a lot of competition since theater is a very specific, highly coveted career path—you'll want to make yourself stand out as the best person for the job.

Your Career in Set Design

If your interest lies in being a professional set designer, be prepared to pare down your interests in order to decide what kind of set designer you want to be. According to professional set designer Ken Larson on his website, setdesigner.biz, there are several types of set design. You might want to design sets for movies or television, rather than theater. If so, you should understand that movie or television set design will likely require you to live where movies and television are made: Los Angeles. If your focus is on set design in theater, you'll want to live in a city that supports a healthy theater culture. New York City is the prime location for a burgeoning theater set designer in the United States. As you make larger decisions about how to pursue your chosen career, you might want to research theaters online or even attend

Professional set designers spend a lot of time with a pencil and paper, planning out productions in order to create the best possible visual experience for the audience.

some performances to get an idea of what kind of theater most interests you.

As for education, an amateur set designer might want to take classes in interior design and art, computer design, or drafting. He or she might want to get a bachelor's degree or an associate's degree in art, interior design, or even architecture. Different employers have different requirements, so if you're interested in set design, be prepared to meet those requirements. Ask people for informational interviews at which you can ask a professional working in the field how he or she achieved success, or check out internship opportunities. The most important thing you can do is to begin networking as soon as you can.

Reach out to people you admire who have your dream job. Talk to people who share your interests. Join a club or an online forum (being sure to protect your identity and safety), and just start researching your chosen path and asking questions.

House Carpenter

In preparation to be a theater's house carpenter, you'll have to train first as a carpenter. You are not required to get a degree, but you'll need to learn through a carpentry apprenticeship or other training program, and then spend a lot of time honing your skills. As a high school student, see if your school has an advanced woodworking program and take some classes. And be prepared to build things! The only way to become a terrific carpenter is to try out some projects and learn from your mistakes. Keep your eyes out for opportunities for novice carpenters. Helping to build a float for the homecoming parade or hanging shelves for a neighbor is a great way to gain some experience.

Props Master

Props masters often start out in entry-level roles and work their way up. If you can prove yourself as a capable props assistant and build your résumé by helping with a lot of successful productions, people will begin to see you as an asset. You can also take art, basic carpentry, or computer classes.

However, the most important skill that you need to prepare yourself for a career in theater is dedication.

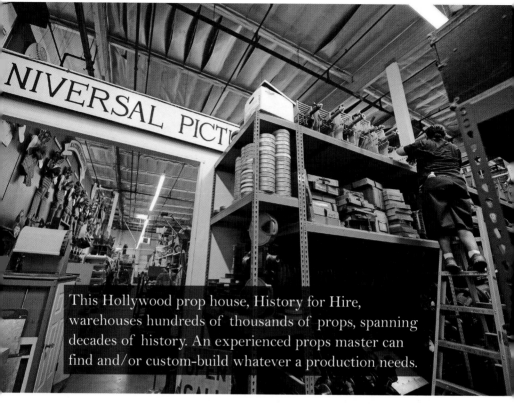

This Hollywood prop house, History for Hire, warehouses hundreds of thousands of props, spanning decades of history. An experienced props master can find and/or custom-build whatever a production needs.

See shows when you can, and keep an eye out for your favorite show features. You never know when inspiration will strike! If you decide to pursue a formal education, you might want to major in history in order to create a level of historical accuracy in the work you do. You can also major in art or film if you would like to pursue a career as a props master in television or the movies.

Beyond the Theater

Even if you don't want to pursue a career working in theater or decide later on that it's not quite for you, your time spent working in theater won't have

YOUR RÉSUMÉ SKILLS

One of the big issues that job seekers encounter while crafting a résumé is finding an effective way to showcase a skill or set of skills. Simply writing that you participated in a theater program in high school and college doesn't give employers a good representation of the experience and the part you played in it. So as you're crafting your résumé to help launch your career in theater, you'll want to be sure of a few specific guidelines.

1. Use active, effective verbs. Let's say you helped build a set for a production of *Into the Woods* during your sophomore year in high school. This is a terrific example of you actively participating in a theater production. So don't just say, "Participated in set building for musical production." Instead write, "Constructed set for musical production as part of a team."

2. Provide detail. The more detail you provide, the more interested a potential employer will be. You don't need to write an essay, but simply writing, "Sourced vintage props for 2014 high school production of *The Importance of Being Earnest*," can help show that you appreciate details and have a great memory for them.

3. Stay organized. If you participated in four years of high school theater productions, you might want to list them in order from most recent to earliest, detailing how you participated each time. That will show the growth of your skills and great dedication to theater and the theater community around you.

been wasted. Experience working on a theater production can set you up with a lot of long-term skills. According to a 2013 article in *Forbes*, the top-ten skills employers are seeking in new employees are the following:

1. Ability to work in a team

2. Ability to make decisions and solve problems

3. Ability to plan, organize, and prioritize work

4. Ability to communicate verbally with people inside and outside an organization

5. Ability to obtain and process information

6. Ability to analyze quantitative data

7. Technical knowledge related to the job

8. Proficiency with computer software programs

9. Ability to create and/or edit written reports

10. Ability to sell and influence others

Being able to show an employer that you possess these skills is as simple as creating an effective résumé that showcases your experience. According to an article on LinkedIn by Goose Creek Consolidated director of fine arts Phillip Morgan, many of these skills can be learned through a terrific theater experience. He says, "Yes, unbeknownst to the masses, theatre actually forces you to learn a lot about mathematics and science. From angles of doorframes for theatrical sets to the complex budgetary equations

OPENING NEW WORLDS

David Gallaher is the writer and co-creator of the *Only Living Boy* graphic novel series. He's worked on projects for a variety of publishers, including Marvel Comics. As he relates in an email interview for this book, high school theater had a huge impact on his life.

Q. What was your experience with theater in high school?

A. Okay, so I started high school in 1989. That first month, I auditioned for *Up the Down Staircase* and got a supporting role. Part of the condition of being an actor in the play is that everybody had to put in ten hours of set time, working with the tech and set crew to build, paint, and wire where needed. I had such a positive experience building sets that the following year, I joined set crew and built sets for *The Mousetrap*, while also carrying a lead role in the play.

One of the things that made set work as enjoyable for me as acting was that it created a strong sense of trust and camaraderie with my teammates. Together, we were all working on shared and common goals. I was a super shy kid, but participating in theater really opened me up and created opportunities for strong friendships.

Q. What skills do you think you gained while participating in the theater program?

A. In terms of practical skills, I learned woodworking and carpentry. I'm no master builder, but to this day

I can still construct and hang a sturdy two-story set, if I have all of the right materials. With learning carpentry, I also learned about the nuances of power tools, and what the right tool for the right job was. All crucial skills for the set work I did throughout high school and college and for all the home repairs in my adult life.

Q. How do you feel those skills apply to your current career path?

A. As a graphic novelist and author, set construction and stagecraft allowed me to better understand how the characters in my stories move. I was able to increase my spatial imagination and I was able to develop nuanced backstories for why props appeared in my narratives. Every prop and every piece of set serves a purpose and should add to the overall tone of the story you're telling.

Q. What advice would you give a student who wants to go into a similar field?

A. "There are no small parts" is a line you'll frequently hear in the theater community. And … it's true. As a member of the stagecraft crew, you're an important part of the story that the cast is telling. As you transition into the next phase of your career, remember that everybody is essential and has a role to play—treating everyone with kindness and respect, no matter who they are or what part they play, will do you well.

that must be established to evaluate a theatre's net worth, math is a standard in the world of drama. Until you've gotten oil-based paint stuck on your favorite jeans, you won't understand how theatre students hypothesize methods of chemical treatment to remove said stain. From algebra to dry ice special effects, theatre encompasses a lot of the STEM."

Dry ice, which is often used to create the illusion of fog during a performance, requires special care and a general understanding of its chemical makeup in order to handle it safely.

So if you're asking yourself, "What kind of career outside of theater can I pursue using my theater skills?" the answer is … *anything*. The possibilities are endless. It might take time, education, networking, trial and error, some failures, some triumphs, late nights and early mornings, and lots and lots of pep talks, but you can fulfill your goals. Theater can help get you there. Eric Hart, the freelance props master, builds props not only for theater productions. He also produces displays for department stores and other retail outlets. Any business that requires workspaces to be laid out with a pleasing effect needs the help of an experienced set designer or props master.

If sets and props aren't your thing, there are a wide variety of other jobs that you can perform better for having worked in theater. The experience will help you manage people, design or create almost anything you want, work on a team, and meet deadlines. You might even invent something for use in theater or other business worlds. In the meantime, get out there and see performances. Talk about what you saw with your friends, and get involved in whatever way you are most comfortable.

Whether or not working in theater is your ultimate goal, almost everything you learn and accomplish can be applied to other parts of your life.

GLOSSARY

arc The structure of a story as the plot builds to a climax and then is resolved.

backdrop Painted scenery used in the place of a more elaborate set to create the illusion of depth.

backstage Any location within a theater where cast and crew work on a performance out of the audience's sight.

breakaway props Props built to break during every performance that can be easily repaired and used again.

budget Money allocated to a particular production or department within a theater.

community theater A theater that is founded and run by a community.

drama club Student club dedicated to staging theatrical productions for a school.

expressionist Subtle, dreamlike, unrealistic set design created to remove characters from reality.

greens Any foliage used for a staged theater production, including trees and flowers.

head carpenter Designer and builder of large set materials, with the help of the crew and under the design direction of the set designer.

models Small representations of a larger item, used in planning and design.

mood The general emotion that a staged piece of work is meant to convey.

niche A job or activity that suits an individual well.

perishable props Props that are consumed or destroyed during each performance and must be replaced each time.

personal props A prop used by an actor, and sometimes chosen by the actor, to help him or her develop a character, such as a cane or pair of glasses.

point of view The position from which an audience member views the stage.

props master Manager of the props department within a theater, who organizes available props and maintains organization of prop objects during a performance.

realism Set design meant to portray the play's action as accurately as possible.

set designer Individual who designs overall mood and tone of a performance through careful planning of items on stage.

set dressing Item or items that are part of a set but aren't used by actors; props and set departments collaborate on set dressing.

set prop A large item, such as a piece of furniture, that remains on the stage and is part of the set, but is technically a prop.

source material The play or musical upon which a production is based.

special effects An illusion used to simulate an imagined event or activity, usually created through the use of technology and ingenuity.

theatricalism Bare-bones set design that relies on the audience's imagination to fill in the details.

theme The underlying subject or idea behind a stage performance.

FOR MORE INFORMATION

Books

Brewster, Karen, and Melissa Shafer. *Fundamentals of Theatrical Design: A Guide to the Basics of Scenic, Costume, and Lighting Design.* New York: Allworth Press, 2011.

Doorley, Scott, and Scott Witthoft. *Make Space: How to Set the Stage for Creative Collaboration.* Hoboken, NJ: Wiley, 2012.

Hart, Eric. *The Prop Building Guidebook: For Theatre, Film, and TV.* Burlington, MA: Focal Press, 2013.

Kaluta, John. *The Perfect Stage Crew: The Complete Technical Guide for High School, College, and Community Theater.* 2nd ed. New York: Allworth Press, 2016.

Maxwell, Richard. *Theater for Beginners.* New York: Theatre Communications Group, 2015.

Mussman, Amy. *The Prop Master: A Guidebook for Successful Theatrical Prop Management.* Colorado Springs, CO: Meriwether Publishing, 2008.

Websites

Architectural Digest
http://www.architecturaldigest.com/celebrity-style/set-design
The *Architectural Digest* warehouses a collection of original set designs from theater, television, and movies for anyone to browse.

The Art Career Project
http://www.theartcareerproject.com/set-design-career/654
This website is a terrific resource for all aspects of finding a career in the arts, from getting the right education to landing a great job.

Eric Hart's Prop Agenda
http://www.props.eric-hart.com_
This website is the go-to props master resource on the internet, filled with anecdotes, advice, and career information from a working props master.

Life as a Stage Carpenter
http://buildingthestagethings.tumblr.com
Run by a working stage carpenter, this blog is filled with photos from backstage at several theater productions and includes a lot of great advice.

Objectively Speaking, It's All About the Prop Master
http://www.npr.org/2011/02/24/134001280/
objectively-speaking-its-all-about-the-prop-master
This NPR profile on working as a props master in the movies is filled with on-the-job anecdotes.

Videos

Practical Technical Theater Demo: Set Design
https://www.youtube.com/watch?v=ahnlcIl-EdM
This three-minute clip from a longer video series about set design takes you into a theater and through a realistic set design to show how the work was done.

Working in the Theatre: Prop Masters
https://www.youtube.com/watch?v=_xWMtFtzRCo
American Theatre Wing follows props masters Kathy Fabian, Buist Bickley, and Faye Armon-Troncoso to find out the ins and outs of what it takes to be a successful props master in the theater.

INDEX

Page numbers in **boldface** are illustrations. Entries in **boldface** are glossary terms.

ABOUT THE AUTHOR

Bethany Bryan is a professional writer, copy editor, editor, and amateur theater enthusiast. She once played a Munchkin in her high school's production of *The Wizard of Oz* and later made her New York stage debut in a production of Eve Ensler's *A Memory, a Monologue, a Rant, and a Prayer.* She has published books with Scholastic, Adams Media, and Rosen Publishing. She lives in North Carolina and loves *Les Misérables* unapologetically.